100 Things

Every Adult College Student
Ought to Know

A self-orientation guide with definitions, customs, procedures,
and advice to assist adults in adjusting to the start of college.

by Carlette Jackson Hardin, Ed.D.
Second Edition

Cambridge Stratford Study Skills Institute
Williamsville, NY

100 Things Every Adult College Student Ought to Know

by Carlette Jackson Hardin, Ed.D

Copyright © 2011 Second Edition
The Cambridge Stratford Study Skills Institute
A division of Cambridge Stratford, Ltd.
8560 Main Street, Williamsville, New York 14221
For information: (716) 626-9044

Library of Congress Control Number: 2011933673
ISBN: 0-935637-35-4   Printed in the USA
Printing is the lowest number: 10 9 8 7 6 5 4 3 2

Drawings by Ellen Klem

Introduction

In the ten years since the first edition of *100 Things Every Adult College Student Ought to Know* was published, much has changed on college campus. Campuses have responded to student needs by providing courses at more convenient times and through alternative formats. Technology is now being use to communicate with students, register for class, and provide course information. Many students never set foot on a college campus but take all their classes online. What has not changed is the number of adult students who make up a large portion of the college population. In fact, upwards of 50% of students on many college campuses today are over the age of twenty-five.

If you haven't been on a college campus lately, you may not know that what was once considered the typical college student has changed drastically. The typical college student is no longer a traditional eighteen-year-old who leaves his/her parents and moves into the college dorm. While such students can still be found on college campuses, they have been joined by adult students who have decided to enter college for the first time or to reenter after an extended absence from academic life. Sitting in class beside teenagers with spiked hair and nose rings, are gray-haired grandmothers. On the intramural fields are teams of forty-year-olds playing against teams from fraternity row.

These adult learners bring experiences to the classroom that add to the wealth of information available to all students. Adult students are described by their instructors as more eager, motivated and committed than traditionally-aged students. Adult students do well in their classes and usually set the curve in most courses. They bring to campus tremendous strengths; their strong desire to learn, their ability to relate their new learning to what they already know, and their ability to use prior experience to find answers to questions that confuse or concern them. Yet, most adult students find that starting college can be filled with confusion. This book can bring clarity.

Unfortunately, traditional-aged students do have one advantage. Because they have had more recent experiences in the classroom, they have a better understanding of the rules, regulations and customs of higher education. This lack of knowledge often creates barriers that adult students find hard to overcome. Often, adult students find they don't know where to go for information and because they leave campus as soon as classes end, they never establish a network of classmates to provide this information. Therefore, adult students find everything from the vocabulary to the administrative structure of the academic environment new and foreign. When adult students often lack information about critical aspects of college, they may hesitate to go back to school or they drop out because they don't know where to go for assistance. Thus, the purpose of *100 Things Adult College Students Ought to Know* is to equip the adult student with the knowledge to make a smoother adjustment to the start of college.

The information for this book was obtained by asking hundreds of adult students, just like you, what were the most important things adult students need to know. They told me that adult students need a way to maneuver around the maze of terms and vocabulary used on a college campuses. Others suggested that adult students needed information so that they could successfully balance their roles of parent, spouse, employee, and student. Some asked for information which would help them become a better student. Additionally, instructors with experience teaching adult learners were asked what things they believed adult learners ought to know. Their comments shed further light on their understanding of the double, triple, and sometimes quadruple roles adult learners must balance to be successful in their academic lives.

The 2nd edition of *100 Things Every Adult College Student Ought to Know* contains six chapters which were in the first edition. These chapters have been updated to provide new information that reflects the changes that have occurred on campuses since the first edition. The first chapter, "Getting Started" provides information about what a student needs to know before enrolling in college. It is designed to help the adult find the best college to fit his/her needs. Also, if planning to transfer in the future, this section may set broad parameters for researching the best choices. The second chapter, "Understanding the Definitions and Customs" highlights some of the unique practices, customs, and definitions used commonly in higher education. It's tied to a convenient glossary listed in the back of the book that will help build your vocabulary as you communicate with campus officials and professors. The third chapter, "Knowing the Turf, Rules, and Players," provides a way of thinking and acting in college. It is based on information that former adult students felt you should know to help you avoid the pitfalls commonly associated with making the adjustment to the start of college. Chapter Four, "Reaching Out," outlines what many students who rush home each day after classes never discover, namely the wealth of services that are available to you beyond the classroom. It also covers some important "do's" for avoiding some of the problems faced by adult students. The fifth chapter, "Gaining Support," outlines how to deal with our prime concern: our existing family, employers and friends and the new network of people who will mold our futures. This chapter will be important in easing your adjustment and communicating with others in your life about your new priority in acquiring a college degree. The sixth chapter, "Studying Smart," offers proven steps that you can take to increase your success. It provides a road map of immediate directions adult students have found to work and opens key topics that can leave you with a wealth of helpful information.

A new chapter has been added to the 2nd edition. Chapter Seven, "Using Technology to Your Advantage," introduces students to the many ways that technology will be used during their college career and the ways it can increase student proficiency. The chapter helps students determine their level of proficiency with technology and additional training they may need. A revised Glossary and alphabetical

Index are also provided at the end to assist you in quickly locating information by topical headings.

I wish to thank the hundreds of adult students who shared their thoughts and insights. I hope this little book makes more than a little impact on your successful adaptation and transition to college. Read it, review it often, and carry it with you during your first term at college. It will become a resource you can use to help navigate your clear path and will provide key tips you can share with family, friends, and college personnel to get the help you need to accomplish your academic goals. Happy reading and good luck as you begin your academic adventure.

Dr. Carlette Jackson Hardin is Professor of Education at Austin Peay State University, Clarksville, Tennessee. She currently serves as Dean for the College of Education. During her thirty year career in higher education, Dr. Hardin has worked extensively with adult students as an advisor, workshop leader, and sponsor of support groups for returning students. Through these interactions, she has learned of the needs, concerns, fears, and goals of adult students. She provides information concerning effective programing and teaching for the adult learner in presentations, inservices, and workshops across the country.

Table of Contents

1 Getting Started

College is not just for the creative or the really smart people. It is for ordinary folks who want to improve their lives.

Michael, 42 years old
English Major

Adult College Students Ought to Know:

1.   that it's **never too late** to follow a dream. If you have always dreamed of going to college or returning to college, it's time to start. In fact, the National Center for Education Statistics notes that there were almost 7 million students enrolled in higher education in 2007 and the number is predicted to climb to over 8 million by 2018. If you attend, you will find lots of students with whom you can relate. Go for it! You won't be alone.

Helpful Website:
http://nces.ed.gov/programs/digest/d09/tables/dt09_191.asp

Adult College Students Ought to Know:

2.   that there is **no need for guilt**. Understand that you are seeking to improve your life through education. The best gift you can give yourself or your family is an education. When you receive your diploma, most everyone will agree that the sacrifices made by you and your family were worth the effort.

Adult College Students Ought to Know:

3.   that it won't help to dwell on what you **should have learned** 10-20 years ago. You can't turn back the clock, but you can make up for lost time. Don't dwell on the past. Determine that starting today you are going to absorb as much knowledge as you can.

Helpful Website:
http://www.ecampustours.com/forparents/collegeplanning/adviceforadultstudents.htm

Adult College Students Ought to Know:

4.   that **past academic records can be erased**. Many adults returning to college may have started as traditional students. However, some may have dropped out due to financial obligations, completing responsibilities, or lack of focus, motivation, and maturity. "I dreaded revealing my grades from my last institution," stated one student. "Then I realized many colleges offer programs to clear up past performances and start fresh." While different terms are used by different institutions, most offer opportunities to make up or erase past academic difficulties. With a clear attitude, a clean state can get you re-started on the right path.

Adult College Students Ought to Know:

5.   that many **institutions provide specialized programs** and trained personnel to work with adult learner needs. Many community colleges that have historically served adult learners have programs and personnel that effectively serve both traditional and non-traditional students. Four-year institutions often dedicate specially trained individuals to handle the needs of adult learners - admission counselors, advisers, financial aid counselors, and coordinators of support programs, and special services. These are designed for your specific needs. Seek out these resources to ease your transitions at the start of college.

Adult College Students Ought to Know:

6.   that many adult **students initially enroll as "Non-Degree Students**." Therefore, if you aren't sure if you want to enroll as a degree-seeking student or if you aren't sure you want to do more than just take a few classes for personal growth, find out if the option of being a "non-degree student" is available to you.   Typically, colleges allow adult students who have a high school diploma, but who haven't attended college previously to register for up to 12 hours before being formally admitted. [Note: if eligible for financial aid, request advice about this option.]

Adult College Students Ought to Know:

7.   that many students can **attend college without ever stepping foot on a college campus**. More and more colleges are bringing class to community and work locations. Check with your employer to see what opportunities are available to you. In fact, many employers reimburse students for courses. In some cases, unions also provide financial help to union members taking courses.

Not only are these courses offered at locations that are convenient, they are often offered at times that allow you to continue with your normal schedule. Evening classes are an ideal way to balance work, family, friends, and college. In addition, many courses are now available online. Check with your campus to see what's available.

Adult College Students Ought to Know:

8.   that entry into college can be a **gradual process**. You don't have to take a full load the first term you attend. Take one course and see how you feel about being in an academic environment. If you are comfortable and successful, you can increase your load the next term.

If you decide to go full-time your first term, don't take too many classes as an effort to make up for lost time. You have taken the right step by getting started, but be realistic. Enroll for the hours you can handle while balancing your family and other responsibilities. It may take a little longer, but the result will be better mental health for you, better relationships with those you love, and better grades overall.

Adult College Students Ought to Know:

9.   that you can **audit courses**. Auditing is like being a listener in a course and receiving no grade. If you are nervous about taking that first course, you might want to audit a course. While payment is usually required, auditing allows you to take a course without the worry of earning a grade. This is a chance to test the waters. Also, a pass/fail grade is an option in some courses. This allows you to complete course requirements without worrying about an "A," "C," etc. Many colleges have restrictions on when you can audit a course and/or if courses are offered with the pass/fail option, so check with your college regarding its policy.

Helpful Website:
http://www.ehow.com/how_2081881_audit-class.html

Adult College Students Ought to Know:

10. that many campuses offer **special orientation sessions or transition courses** for adult students. Attend!

The orientation sessions will provide valuable information about the campus. You will have a chance to meet other adult students who are going through the same struggles and challenges as you. Many times such sessions offer an opportunity for students to register for classes in a more relaxed atmosphere and meet professors who can provide details and assistance.

Campuses often offer transition courses sometimes referred to as College Survival, Freshman Seminars, University 101, or similar titles. Enrollment during your first or second term can help you overcome many of the adjustment problems associated with starting college. Once enrolled, you will meet others making the same transition and learn that you are not alone in your feelings, attitudes, skills, or needs. These courses have been proven to improve students' academic skills and success in college.

Adult College Students Ought to Know:

11. that they have several choices in **choosing a post-secondary institution**. Institutions fall into one of four types, each with advantages and disadvantages. Your individual needs, circumstances, and educational requirements will assist you in deciding which is best for you. These four types are:

a.   Two-year colleges - Sometimes called community colleges, these schools tend to emphasize vocational, pre-professional, and job-oriented courses. Many offer two-year liberal arts program transferable to a four-year institution. Two-year community colleges typically have a slightly older student body, and they cater to the needs of these students by providing courses on nights and weekends. They are often less expensive than four-year colleges. In addition, classes tend to be smaller at two-year schools.

    b.   Public colleges and universities - Because these institutions receive public funding, they provide quality education at reasonable prices. A variety of majors are offered. However, not all majors are offered at all institutions, so be sure to inquire about the major you desire.

c.   Private college and universities - Some of these institutions carry more prestige than public institutions, but also carry higher fees. They often emphasize quality education that meets individualized needs with smaller classes and specialized majors.

d.   Technical and vocational schools - These schools offer specialized training in a variety of fields. The emphasis is on job training. If your desire is to enter the job market quickly, a vocational diploma may serve you well. If your desire is to have a career which allows you more upward mobility, a more traditional degree may be what you want.

Helpful Websites:

http://www.collegeview.com/articles/CV/application/two-vs-four-years.html

http://www.collegeconfidential.com/dean/archives/000294.htm

http://collegesearch.collegeboard.com/search/adv_typeofschool.jsp

Adult College Students Ought to Know:

12. that **not all institutions are accredited**. Therefore, the coursework at these institutions is not recognized by some companies or acceptable for transfer to other institutions.   Be sure to ask about the type of accreditation of the institution and the transferability of the coursework to other institutions.

This advice is more critical today than ever before. With the increase of online degrees, many students are learning that the degree they earned is not valued by employers or that their coursework is not transferable. Make sure that the institution, degree, or program is accredited before enrolling in the first course. Coursework is too expensive to learn that it can't be used to obtain a job or earn a degree.

Helpful Websites:
http://www.accreditedonlinecolleges.com/
http://ope.ed.gov/accreditation/

Adult College Students Ought to Know:

13. that many colleges give **credit for life experiences and credit by examination**. You may be eligible for degree credit for previous work experience or other activities. This is sometimes called life experience credit. Some institutions require the student to present a prior learning portfolio. This is a written record presented by the student requesting college credit for learning outside the classroom. Credit is given only for college-level learning, and the portfolio must be well documented and organized. Your institution will provide details on how the portfolio should be presented.

You may earn credit on the basis of your performance on specified examinations. These exams can be the college's own challenge examinations or those of the College-Level Examination Program (CLEP). Discuss these options with your admissions counselor. The experiences you've had before attending college may speed your goal of earning a degree. [Note: credit received may not count toward your Grade Point Average and may not be transferable to another college.]

Helpful Websites:

http://www.back2college.com/library/test.htm

http://www.collegescholarships.org/blog/2009/04/29/
getting-college-credit-for-life-experience-it-can-be-done/

http://professionals.collegeboard.com/higher-ed/placement/
clep/advise/adult-students

Adult College Students Ought to Know:

14. that every institution **publishes a catalog** of its academic programs, policies, procedures, and course descriptions. These catalogs are also called bulletins at some institutions. Before enrolling at any institution, request a catalog. Check admissions policies. Find out about the accreditation of the institution. Determine if the institution has the major you desire, or if not, prepares you to transfer to an institution that does.

Once you enroll, keep the catalog. Unless an external, outside accrediting or licensing group changes a requirement which forces a change in your program, most institutions allow you to graduate under the requirements listed in the catalog in place when you entered. A curriculum check-sheet is often available listing all requirements needed to attain your degree. Get one early. While there is typically a time limit on how long one has to complete a degree under a specific catalog, this policy will protect you if for some reason you must take a leave from school.

If you leave the institution, keep the catalog. If you decide to transfer, the catalog will provide a description of the courses you took and assist you in earning transfer credit.

Adult College Students Ought to Know:

15. that many **different titles** are used to describe adult learners. They may be called "adult learners," "non-traditional students," "mature students," "returning students," "older students," or "adult students." Whatever the title, adult students are defined as juggling many different roles and responsibilities with work, family or community commitments. They are electing to juggle into their mix of responsibilities, the role of college student. This is an act of a highly motivated person. You should be proud to join their ranks as you bring valuable experience to share with other students in each classroom.

Helpful Websites:
http://www.nontradstudents.com/
http://adulted.about.com/od/intro/u/
Nontradstudentpath.htm
http://www.adultstudentcenter.com/
http://www.collegeforadults.org/

Activity 1
Selecting the Right School for You

List two or three schools you are considering attending. For each item, check if the school meets your needs.

Needs	School One	School Two	School Three
Convenient to work and home	_____	_____	_____
Courses offered at convenient times	_____	_____	_____
Offers degree I want to earn	_____	_____	_____

Needs	School One	School Two	School Three
Offers option to remove past records	_____	_____	_____
Allows students to enroll as "non-degree"	_____	_____	_____
Provides option to audit courses	_____	_____	_____
Courses available			
Where I work	_____	_____	_____
Via Internet	_____	_____	_____
Via TV	_____	_____	_____

Needs	School One	School Two	School Three
Provides services for adult students	_____	_____	_____
Is accredited	_____	_____	_____
Accepts credit for			
Life Experiences	_____	_____	_____
Military Credit	_____	_____	_____
Testing	_____	_____	_____

Based on the above assessment, where would you enroll?

No goal is unattainable.

Adult students are often confused by the jargon of academic life.

Understanding the Definitions and Customs

2

Adult students ought to know that being homecoming queen is not an option.

Marla
35 year old Sophomore

Adult College Students Ought to Know:

16. that **each campus has its own list of definitions and terms**.   Often acronyms are used such as PIN (Personal Identification Number) or SID (Student Identification Number). It may seem that colleges have their own language and that you have entered a foreign country. Don't be afraid to ask what a term means. It may save you time and frustration if you do. A glossary of the most common terms used on many campuses appears at the end of this book. Review it. You'll begin to feel more comfortable when you can use these terms in discussions with faculty, staff, and fellow students.

Adult College Students Ought to Know:

17. that they will use a **student identification number** every time they do anything official with the institution. The institution will provide this number for you. Be sure to learn this number as you will be asked for it often. Until you can remember the number, you might want to store it on your cell phone.

Adult College Students Ought to Know:

18. that the **definition of an academic year varies** from institution to institution. The typical year begins with the opening of classes each August or September through final examinations and graduation in the spring. Commonly, the academic year consists of two semesters or three quarters, followed by an additional summer session (with possible short intercessions) of course offerings. Your college catalog or bulletin will provide these dates.

Adult College Students Ought to Know:

19. the **importance of having an Academic Advisor**. The academic advisor is usually a faculty or staff member who advises the student about his or her academic program.   However, advisors serve a much more important function than simply signing your course request form. Besides being able to advise you what specific courses you must take, they know all about your major and the requirements for graduation. They know other professors and can direct you to professors who will match your learning style. They can help you find internships and serve as a reference when you apply for job. They will help you

analyze options for careers after graduation. In addition, they are often available to provide important personal advice.

Always make an appointment before going to see your advisor. This will ensure that you will have your advisor's undivided attention. Also, go to your advisor with a list of questions.

You can delay your graduation if you miss a course that isn't offered every semester, especially if it's required (a prerequisite) before taking other courses you need. Have your advisor review your program periodically to see that you are on track for graduation.

Helpful Websites:
http://www.collegeview.com/articles/CV/campuslife/academic_advisor.html

http://www.completecollegeplanning.net/what-to-ask-your-academic-adviser.php

Adult College Students Ought to Know:

20. that you should make an **advising notebook**. In this notebook, keep a copy of your degree checklist and mark off courses as you take them. Keep all correspondence concerning degree completion. If you request a substitution for a course, keep a copy of the request and the written approval for your records. Having all these records in one place will make your life less stressful when it comes time to apply for graduation.

Adult College Students Ought to Know:

21. about the **value of remedial and developmental courses**. Too often adult students avoid remedial or developmental courses for fear that these courses will delay graduation. In reality, these courses can speed graduation because they not only provide students skills to pass future courses, but they provide skills so that students succeed academically. If you are advised to take such courses, realize that you are being given an opportunity to do your very best in school.

Adult College Students Ought to Know:

22. and understand how students are **classified at their institutions**. Classification indicates the level of progress you have made toward your degree. Typically, undergraduate students are classified as freshmen until they have earned 24 hours. They are classified as sophomores when they have earned between 25 and 59 hours. Students become juniors when they have earned 60 hours. Once you are classified as a senior (at around 85 hours) you will remain so until graduation. Check specific classifications at your college.

Adult College Students Ought to Know:

23. that certain courses have **corequisites or prerequisites**. A course which must be taken at the same time as another course is called a corequisite. A requirement which must be met before enrolling in particular courses is called a prerequisite. These corequisites and prerequisites are required to make sure you have the skills needed to be successful in the course. Therefore, before enrolling in any course, check to see if the course has corequisites or prerequisites.

Adult College Students Ought to Know:

24. that **each course carries a certain amount of credit** which will add to the total credits required for graduation. Generally, a course meeting one hour a week through a semester carries one semester-hour credit, a course meeting two hours a week carries two semester-hour credits, and so on. The number of courses you take may be more important than the number of credits. Four courses worth sixteen credits may be more manageable than five courses worth fifteen credits.

Approximately 120 credits are required for a bachelor's degree, and at least 60 credits are required for an associate degree. Colleges operating on a quarter calendar use a similar system based on quarter-hour credits, with 3 quarter-hour credits usually equivalent to 2 semester-hour credits.

Adult College Students Ought to Know:

25. how to **calculate their grade point average (GPA)**. The GPA is a numerical index of overall student academic performance. It is calculated by first multiplying the number of credits earned in each completed course by the numerical value of the student's grade in that course (generally A=4, B=3, C=2, D=1, and F=0). All the resulting grade points for each course are then added, and their sum is divided by the total number of credits attempted. For example, a student who has earned "A's" in all courses will have a GPA of 4.0. Some grades will not

count in the calculation of the GPA. Check to see how grades count at your institution.

Helpful Websites:
http://www.back2college.com/gpa.htm
http://www.youtube.com/watch?v=VhLMTaExzOs

Adult College Students Ought to Know:

26. that **course numbering** indicates the level of course offered. Courses which are numbered in the 100's (or 1000) or 200's (or 2000) are usually freshman and sophomore level courses. Junior and senior level course are usually in the 300's (or 3000) and 400's (or 4000). Graduate courses are typically numbered 500 (or 5000) and above. Check your registration to make sure you are not taking courses at an inappropriate level. If you take courses at too high a level, you may not have the appropriate background to succeed in the course. If you take courses at too low a level, you may not get the credit you need for graduation. Be sure to have your advisor check the courses you wish to take.

Adult College Students Ought to Know:

27. that your institution will require you to take a **certain number of hours to be considered a full-time student**. At most institutions, this number is twelve semester hours. You may be required to be a full-time student in order to receive all the services provided by the institution. Typically, full-time student status is required for student housing. Full-time status may also be required for some types of financial assistance.

However, you must be careful that you don't register for a full load if you don't have the time to give to meet all the demands of school, home, and work. If you are working full-time, you are setting yourself up for failure if you also try to be a full-time student. If your family obligations will prevent you from devoting the hours you will need for study, you might want to attend part-time. Most faculty recommend that you plan to spend two to three hours outside class for each hour you are in class. Therefore, a twelve credit hour load equates to 24 to 36 hours of out of class work each week. Be realistic about your ability to handle this amount of work.

Adult College Students Ought to Know:

28. what **type of program or degree they want to earn**. A variety of programs and degrees are offered by most institutions and include:

• Certificates Programs—These programs are designed for students who need to update their work skills, acquire new skills, or change careers. They are shorter programs and can typically take anywhere from eight weeks to a year to complete. Find out before starting a certificate program if you can use the credits earned toward an associate or bachelor's degree if you decide to pursue a degree at a later time.

• Associate's Degree—This type of degree requires about 60 credit hours of study and is often offered at a community college. Many students who complete an associate's degree program often transfer into a bachelor's degree program.

• Bachelor's Degree—The bachelor's degree is the most popular of all the degree programs and is earned at a college or university. Students pursuing a bachelor's degree must complete between 120 and 128 credit hours.

Ask your advisor or someone from the admissions office to explain the types of degrees available at your institution.

Helpful Websites:
http://www.smartaboutcollege.org/get-to-college/college-degree-types.jsp
http://www.online-degrees-today.com/content/types-of-college-degrees-online.shtml
http://www.bachelordegrees.net/bachelor/types-of-degrees.asp

Adult College Students Ought to Know:

29. that **career counseling and job placement services are available**. Career counseling can help you decide which academic direction to take for the career you desire. Interest inventories, values assessments, and career decision advice are services that career counselors can provide. Job placement services are also available to college students including resume writing support, job hunting technique, and interviewing skill building. Look for these services at your institution.

Activity 2   Planning Your Degree

Using your school catalog, list all courses you will need to take to complete your degree each term until you complete your degree. Remember that you may need to make changes based on course availability. If you need assistance, check with your academic adivisor.

1. List all courses that you will transfer from another institution, and/or earn through military credit or testing.

    _____   _____

    _____   _____

    _____   _____

    _____   _____

2. Determine during which terms you will take the remaining courses for your degree.

Term 1	Term 2	Term 3	Term 4
_____	_____	_____	_____
_____	_____	_____	_____
_____	_____	_____	_____
_____	_____	_____	_____
_____	_____	_____	_____

Term 5   Term 6   Term 7   Term 8

_____   _____   _____   _____

_____   _____   _____   _____

_____   _____   _____   _____

_____   _____   _____   _____

_____   _____   _____   _____

Knowing the Turf, Rules, and Players

Take a few minutes after class to have a cup of coffee with a classmate. Not only will it allow you to network and find help with your school work, you might gain a new friend that will enrich your life long after you earn your degree.

Sandra, mother of eight
One semester from graduation

Adult College Students Ought to Know:

30. that **learning the ropes**, the characteristics of fellow students who climb them, and what obstacles you'll face on the way up, will make adjusting to the task easier. Give careful consideration to the points that follow. Use them to understand how your special needs can be met as you climb toward your college degree.

Adult College Students Ought to Know:

31. that **asking for help is the critical first step** in enabling others to help you. When you have a problem, go to your instructor, your advisor, or the counselor at your institution who works with adult students. They not only want to help you because they have a personal commitment to see that you meet your goals — it's their job. Whenever you are facing an issue that might mean you can't continue your education or whenever you are discouraged, seek these people out. They know where students just like you go for assistance.

Adult College Students Ought to Know:

32. that **every student comes to campus with specific goals, fears, and misconceptions**. Traditional age students often think that adult students have an edge over them. They mistakenly think that adult students have lots of time to study and are in bed by 9:00. They assume that adult students will set the curve and make earning a good grade harder for everyone. Adult students also have misconceptions about traditional students. They assume that since traditional age students have

been in a classroom more recently, they know how to study. They think that traditional students have lots of time because they don't have to juggle school, work, and family. The truth is that non-traditional students and traditional students have lots in common. Many traditional students are single parents, having the same struggles as their adult counterparts. Most adult students work hard for their grades and have to burn the midnight oil to make the curve. Take time to get to know all students.

Adult College Students Ought to Know:

33. that **adult students are returning to college for a variety of reasons**. When questioned, adult students list the following three reasons for returning to college: 1) a desire for a career change, 2) a change in life-style due to divorce, retirement, or company downsizing, and 3) a desire to reach a lifetime dream of completing a degree. Locate other adult students with similar goals. Having the support of those who share your dreams and goals will help you over the hurdles you face.

Adult College Students Ought to Know:

34. that feeling uncomfortable and "left out" is a **temporary phenomenon**. As you've found in joining groups in the past, assimilation is a product of time on task. As you hang around after class to talk to classmates and interact with your professors, you will feel more comfortable. You'll build a direct connection to new friends and help-providers. It will help to find a "been there" classmate. Their adjustment experiences can be helpful and a positive reinforcement for you.

Adult College Students Ought to Know:

35. that **your concerns are REAL**. Don't ignore them! Face up to them, and seek help. For instance, do you have trouble balancing work, family, friends, and study? Are you concerned about child care?   Are you concerned about underdeveloped study and computer skills or a lack of time?   Or are you experiencing difficulty fitting into the institution's policies, procedures, customs, and practices? Talk to your advisor about your concerns. You may be surprised by the resources available to you.

Adult College Students Ought to Know:

36. that learning and class success can be improved by understanding the value of a **"study partner" or "study group."** You can learn more when you learn collaboratively with others. Find study partners in each class with whom you can share notes, talk about what you have learned, and quiz each other for tests.

Study groups can also play a large part in your success because:

a. study groups increase your academic success. By comparing and contrasting course notes, covering for one another when one of you can't attend class, and generally watching out for one another's interest, group members provide a rich resource for academic success. In addition, a group provides you with multiple views on what's important. A group helps clarify what you don't understand.

b.   study groups represent multiple learning styles. In a group, another student's learning style may better match the instructor's teaching style. Discussions might clarify some points you are having trouble grasping.

c.   study groups are a source of friends. Members of groups have common goals and concerns. Group members encourage each other and don't allow small failures to become big issues. They provide important support for one another. You will probably discover that you share other interests as well.

Adult College Students Ought to Know:

37. that you **need to balance the dream with reality**. The average grade earned in courses is a "C," not an "A." Most students earn lower grades than they want during the first term as they get readjusted to being in a school environment. Too often, these realities cause undue stress on adult students as they allow the desire for earning academic honors to get in the way of enjoying the experience of being a student. Upon graduating it won't matter if you have earned a 3.0 or 4.0 GPA. Your degree, coupled with your life experience, will be the most important factors an employer considers as you start or change careers.

Adult College Students Ought to Know:

38.   that, when possible, **courses and professors should be selected with care**. Too often, adult students select courses and professors based on when the course is offered rather than if they need the course or if the course is taught in a way that matches their learning style. Never take courses just because they are at a convenient time. Only take courses that are required for your program. Otherwise, you will be delaying your degree and filling your transcripts with electives you did not need. When you have a choice in professors, talk to your advisor and fellow students to learn how the course is taught. If the professor teaches in a fashion that matches your learning style, you will find the course work easier and more exciting.

Adult College Students Ought to Know:

39. that **difficult courses and professors are unavoidable**.
Typically each major has certain courses that have a reputation
of being difficult. When you have a term in which you must
take a difficult course, you may want to cut back the number of
courses you take or other obligations you have. However, don't
be surprised if your perception of a difficult course or professor
is different from that of your classmates. You may find the
course exciting and challenging.

Activity 3
What is Important to You in Course Selection?

Put a check in the proper column that best describes your wants and desires for each item listed.

Item	Very Important	Important	Not Important
Time of Day course is offered	_____	_____	_____
Ability to establish a personal relationship with Instructor	_____	_____	_____

Item	Very Important	Important	Not Important
Instruction Delivery:			
Lecture Format	_____	_____	_____
Discussion Format	_____	_____	_____
Hands-on Format	_____	_____	_____
Self-Paced Format	_____	_____	_____
Use of visuals	_____	_____	_____
Imput from Students:			
Student Discussion	_____	_____	_____
Student Presentations	_____	_____	_____

Item	Very Important	Important	Not Important
Grading:			
Based on tests alone	_____	_____	_____
Based on student projects, no tests	_____	_____	_____
Based on combination of tests and projects	_____	_____	_____
Based on point system or percentage	_____	_____	_____
Based on pre-set curve	_____	_____	_____

Item	Very Important	Important	Not Important
Teacher Personality:			
High Energy	_____	_____	_____
Reserve, Serious	_____	_____	_____
Humorous, Storyteller	_____	_____	_____
Content Driven	_____	_____	_____
Well Organized	_____	_____	_____
Type of Test:			
Objective Test–T/F, Multiple Choice, etc.	_____	_____	_____
Subjective Tests–Essay, Discussion Questions	_____	_____	_____

Item	Very Important	Important	Not Important
Outside Assistance:			
Teacher available for tutoring	_____	_____	_____
Tutoring available throught individuals, labs, etc.	_____	_____	_____
Teacher generated study groups	_____	_____	_____
Student generated study groups	_____	_____	_____

Item	Very Important	Important	Not Important
Expectations:			
Expectations given at beginning of course	_____	_____	_____
Expectations flexible based on time restraints and student interests	_____	_____	_____

Now list the items you marked "Very Important." Rearrange these items in priority order with the item you consider the most important as #1. Once you complete this list, you know the characteristics you desire in a course and an instructor. Use this list when you talk to your advisor about the best course for you.

Sometimes the demands of college can seem overwhelming.

Reaching Out

Adult students ought to know that frozen pizza won't kill your family.

Kim,
35 year old freshman

Adult College Students Ought to Know:

40. that **campus resources are available** to them. When you know what needs you have, find out what campus resources are available to help you. Get a list from our college catalog or student service bulletin. Then, reach out. Consider visiting each office. You might discover that there is free tutoring available for adult students. Often writing, reading, computer, and math labs are available to assist you. Counseling, internships, adult student activity clubs, and part-time employment services may be available. Services are available and designed for you. Check them out, early!

Adult College Students Ought to Know:

41. that **campus housing is often available** for adults, single parents, or couples.   Campus housing is reasonably priced, convenient to classes, and protected by campus security. This may be an option you will want to consider.

Single adult students often avoid student housing because they don't want to live in the typical dorm rooms offered to students.   However, other options may be available.   Many residential campuses have apartment options at a cost which is much less than living off campus. Honor dorms often house more mature students who want to be in a dorm that emphasizes academics rather than partying. If your only option is a traditional dorm, find out if you can pay a little extra for a private room.

While not all schools offer housing for adult students, many have referral services to assist you in finding cost effective, convenient housing options. Be sure to ask.

Adult College Students Ought to Know:

42. that most campuses **provide some type of health services to students**. These services are not restricted to students who live on campus. For the most part, only basic routine care is given. In many cases, services which aren't provided free are provided at a greatly reduced price. Visit your institution's health office. In an emergency, you'll be glad to know where it is located.

Student health insurance is available for students. This insurance will provide medical care at greatly reduced prices.

Adult College Students Ought to Know:

43. that many campuses **provide a gym for their students**. While enrolled, you will be able to use the equipment found at expensive health clubs at no additional cost. Think about taking an hour each day to work on the weight machines, run on the track, or swim. Such activity will greatly reduce your stress level. Check into intramural teams. Not only are these teams a great way to keep in shape, you will make new friends.

Adult College Students Ought to Know:

44. that the first time you **register for courses** can be a frustrating process. Therefore, take advantage of the help provided through orientation programs or by your advisor. Be patient. Many adult students believe that if you can get through your first registration process; the rest of the semester is a snap. After you register for the first term, you will find that the process becomes much easier and you will be able to save time and frustration.

Adult College Students Ought to Know:

45. the **important dates** for the semester. Such dates are the days for advisement, registration, dropping courses, adding courses, mid-terms, and exams. These dates often appear on the institution's Website. Put these dates on a master schedule for the semester.

Adult College Students Ought to Know:

46. that you should **make copies of everything**. These copies can be paper copies or electronic files of your paperwork. Make copies of all papers turned into offices on campus and all major papers turned in to instructors. Campus personnel are human and they deal with hundreds of students each day. Unfortunately, in the process of dealing with all these people, things can get lost. If you have copies of your materials, you will be less frustrated if something gets lost and you can speed up the completion of your paperwork.

Keep copies of course syllabi. If at some point you transfer to another institution, course syllabi can be used to show the material you covered in a particular course.

Adult College Students Ought to Know:

47. that your campus I.D. can save you money at **businesses that give discounts to students**. The office of Student Services can give you a listing of businesses that offer such discounts. Be sure to ask when you go to restaurants and stores if they provide student discounts. Learn about how to get your campus ID. This is critical.

Adult College Students Ought to Know:

48.   there may be **places to buy your texts other than the campus bookstore**. Many times, off-campus booksellers provide texts at greatly reduced prices.   These businesses also purchase used textbooks.

Many textbooks can now be bought online at greatly reduced prices. Make sure that the book you buy is the edition of the text that will be used in your class.

Be sure to check the bulletin boards around campus for the names of other students who want to sell their texts, computers, or calculators.

Adult College Students Ought to Know:

49. that they should **check into possible financial aid**, even if they think they don't qualify. You might be surprised. Financial aid may include grants, loans, and/or student work programs. Eligibility is influenced by many factors, so you may meet the criteria. You may discover that there are scholarships available for adult students. Many local clubs and organizations offer scholarships to adult students.

Remember, the early bird gets the worm when it comes to financial aid. As soon as you determine that you are going to college, visit the financial aid office on your campus. Complete the paperwork needed to acquire financial aid quickly and return it to the campus office. Don't forget to make a copy for your records.

Useful Websites:
http://www.back2college.com/library/finad.htm
http://www.braintrack.com/financial-aid-articles/articles/non-traditional-students

Adult College Students Ought to Know:

50.   that many campuses provide **special services to students who are veterans**.   Such services might include funding for courses, tutoring, etc.   If you feel you qualify for these services, find out if there is an office on your campus that works with veterans.   Many campuses have organizations for veterans that provide support when they enter college.

Helpful Websites:
http://www.gibill.va.gov/
http://www.collegescholarships.org/scholarships/veterans.htm
http://www2.ed.gov/programs/triovub/index.html

Adult College Students Ought to Know:

51. that most campuses offer **special services to students who have disabilities**. If you feel you qualify, ask whom you should see on your campus. This person can help arrange appropriate services or accommodations for you.

Helpful Websites:
http://www2.ed.gov/about/offices/list/ocr/transition.html
http://www.educationquest.org/swd.asp

Adult College Students Ought to Know:

52. the importance of having **reliable transportation**. Keep your car in good shape and just in case your best laid plans go astray, find someone who will be willing to give you a ride. As a backup plan to your back up plan, learn the bus routes. Also check out parking availability, cost, and safety. Consider a car pool of study partners who discuss classes and quiz each other while commuting.

Adult College Students Ought to Know:

53. that on most campuses a **parking decal** only gives the privilege to hunt for a space. Give yourself plenty of time for the daily search for a parking place. Failure to find a parking place can cause you to be late for class and impact your academic success. Talk with classmates. They may have the scoop on cheap, alternative parking. Also, campus parking tickets must be paid. Graduation, transcripts, etc., can be withheld due to unpaid tickets.

Adult College Students Ought to Know:

54. that they should **create a realistic and reasonable budget**. No other problem creates as much stress, anxiety, and worry as not having enough money. As you plan to attend college, include all family members in the discussion and consider the following:

Itemize Your Expenses: Some expenses you had before attending college might be eliminated while new expenses will occur.

Itemize Your Resources: Consider the money you have on hand. Consider sources of grants, loans, and scholarships you will earn.

Construct Your Budget: Determine time periods (as academic or calendar year) and establish a monthly/quarterly expense sheet. Review the budget to see what can be eliminated or how expenses can be cut.

Keep Careful Records: Save all receipts. In some cases, expenses may be tax deductible.

Plan For The Unexpected: Have a cushion so that you can afford the calculators, workbooks, study guides, etc. that your instructors recommend. Have a nest egg for the car repairs, doctors' bills, and other emergencies you weren't expecting.

Adult College Students Ought to Know:

55. that they should think of attending **college as a job**. Therefore, establish hours you will attend and try to get everything done while on campus. If you have children, you'll find it best to stay on campus and study while your children are at day care or in school. You will find fewer distractions in the campus library than at your home. Study at home as little as possible. You will feel calmer and your family will have less resentment about time you spend studying.

Adult College Students Ought to Know:

56. if your campus has **day care**. Campuses often offer day care at a reduced rate for students, faculty, and staff. In addition, some campus day care facilities take drop-ins on an emergency basis. One overlooked advantage of campus day care is that the curriculum of campus day care facilities have often been developed by the education faculty of the campus. This means that the day care your family attends will have the very best in an educational program at very little cost. Before starting school, check the rates and policies.

Many male students don't realize that they qualify for child care as well. Whether you are a married or a single parent, campus child care is something you should explore. You may save time and money.

Some organizations provide day care free to single parents continuing their education. Check whether this is available to you.

Adult College Students Ought to Know:

57. that many institutions **provide work opportunities for students**.   Check with your institution's financial aid and placement offices for work opportunities. Many campus offices have found adult workers to be excellent student workers because of the maturity and work experience they bring to the job.

There are many advantages to working on campus. One, the office personnel understand that students need to study and will allow you to study if they don't have an assignment for you. They understand if you need to rearrange your schedule so that you can study for a test. Two, the office personnel know the campus.   Therefore, they will know to whom you should talk to if you have a problem or concern. Three, student workers may be able to register before other students. If this option is offered, it will allow you to register for courses that typically close early.

Other employment opportunities may include peer counseling, peer tutoring, and peer assistance programs. Hourly wage and tuition stipends may be available.   Adult learners bring tremendous experience and leadership skills to their college community and can help other students in a positive way.

Adult College Students Ought to Know:

58. that if they work, they will need to **maintain a balance between work and school**. Most adult students find it impossible to work full-time and go to school full-time. Therefore, it may be necessary to attend only part-time as long as you have a full-time job. A full academic course load on most campuses is twelve semester hours. While this may seem like very few hours and that you would have plenty of time to work and go to school, it's important to remember that for every hour that you have in class, there will be additional hours for reading, study, and assignments.

Talk to your employer about your plans to continue your education. Reassure your employer that you will continue to take your work seriously and do not plan to let your coursework get in the way of your job. Most employers are very supportive and may be willing to adjust work schedules to accommodate your needs. You might also find that your employer provides tuition assistance to employees.

Often students who work are forced to choose between school and work because of a change in work hours or assignments. Talk to your instructors before deciding how to deal with this change. Sometimes an instructor is teaching the same course at another hour which might work with your schedule.

Activity 4
What Campus Services Do You Need?

Put a check before the campus services you need. Then find the location, contact person, and telephone number for each service you have listed.

	Campus Services	Campus Location	Contact Person	Phone Number
__ Campus Housing	_____	_____	_____	_____
__ Health Services	_____	_____	_____	_____
__ Campus Gym	_____	_____	_____	_____

	Campus Services	Campus Location	Contact Person	Phone Number
__ Campus Post Office	_____	_____	_____	_____
__ Computer Services	_____	_____	_____	_____
__ Campus Bookstore	_____	_____	_____	_____
__ Off-Campus Bookstore	_____	_____	_____	_____
__ Financial Aid	_____	_____	_____	_____
__ Campus Day Care	_____	_____	_____	_____
__ Job Placement Office	_____	_____	_____	_____

	Services	Location	Contact Person	Phone Number
__ Veteran's Services	_____	_____	_____	_____
__ Disabled Services	_____	_____	_____	_____
__ Parking Services	_____	_____	_____	_____
__ Academic Advisement	_____	_____	_____	_____
__ _____	_____	_____	_____	_____
__ _____	_____	_____	_____	_____
__ _____	_____	_____	_____	_____
__ _____	_____	_____	_____	_____

Adult students must juggle many roles.

Gaining Support

If you want your children to read, read in front of them. If you want your children to study, study with them. If you want your children to go to college, enroll in college. As parents, we have to walk the walk and talk the talk.

Richard, second semester freshman
Father of three

Adult College Students Ought to Know:

59. that you are becoming a **role model** for all your family, friends, and fellow employers. What you are doing is worthy of respect . . . and you will get it. The tone you set by prioritizing your time and study responsibilities will become a model for others to follow. Don't be surprised if others follow your lead by reading a book or magazine during your study time. Some may wish to go to the library with your or sit in on a class. The more disciplined you become, the more they'll follow your lead.

Adult College Students Ought to Know:

60. the **first semester is going to be tough**. Most college graduates say it is the toughest of all. It will take you a while to get your bearings. Don't get discouraged. You will soon have a routine, your family will have adjusted, and you will be on your way to achieving your dream.

Adult College Students Ought to Know:

61. the **importance of family support**. Family support can be the difference in your success or failure.   Therefore, it is important that your family supports your decision to attend college. While excited at first, resentment can develop as you have less time for the family and responsibilities have to be redistributed. Therefore, you should hold family meetings to discuss issues and concerns. Early topics include being realistic about the financial and personal sacrifices that will be necessary in order for you to attend college. These meetings can keep little issues from becoming big problems.   Make sure everyone understands the long-term benefits for a short time sacrifice.

Adult College Students Ought to Know:

62. that family members will be more comfortable about you attending college if they know where you will be each day. Plan a **family tour** of the campus. Show them the buildings and classrooms you will be using. Allow your family to have a mental picture of where you will spend your days and/or evenings.

This is also an excellent time for you to visit each building and determine how long it will take to walk from building to building. Determine where the bathrooms, elevators, and stairs are in each building. Take your tour when the campus isn't crowded and you aren't rushed. You will feel more comfortable on your first day and so will your family.

Adult College Students Ought to Know:

63. that they need to **get their families involved**. Bring your family to campus events. Have a picnic on the campus lawn. If your family feels a part of your academic experience, they will have less resentment about the time you spend away from them. Also, exposing children to college facilities can impact their futures. Studies indicated that children exposed to college campuses early have a better potential to attend.

If resentment occurs, find ways to deal with it quickly. Don't ignore it. Investigate coping skills and remember that counselors are available. Workshops or panel discussions hosted by seasoned adult learners may be offered. Be sure to attend. If you feel guilty, abused, or question whether you're neglecting those around you, find what has worked for others. Adjustment to change is normal. Learn how to adjust, stay focused and help others help you.

Adult College Students Ought to Know:

64. that a great way to motivate school age children is **do your homework with them**. Study time becomes quality time and shows children the importance of school work.

Adult College Students Ought to Know:

65. the importance of **quality time with your family**. Once a week, have an evening when everyone is together. Sit at the dinner table and share your week's experiences. Go out to eat and enjoy a movie. Take the children to the park. Everyone will have a lot to talk about and it will give everyone a dedicated time to catch up on things.

Adult College Students Ought to Know:

66. the **importance of saying "No!"** With the added burdens of school, you won't be able to do all you did before becoming a student. It may be time to give up some activities. If you try to do all things, you won't give 100% to anything. Establish your priorities!

Adult College Students Ought to Know:

67. that **no one has the right to ask you to choose school over family needs**. If a faculty member, administrator, or staff person tries to suggest otherwise, remember that only you can determine what needs to be a priority for your time.

Adult College Students Ought to Know:

68. that **reliable childcare is critical**. Have a back-up system for emergencies. Know who you will call if your care provider is unable to take care of your child. Know what you will do if your school-age child has to miss a day of school. A missed day of school may not be critical for your second grader, but it can be the difference between passing and failing for you.

Adult College Students Ought to Know:

69. it's sometimes great to encourage **their "significant others" to take a course**. Even if the person you love has a degree, he/she can probably find a "fun" course to take. You can travel to campus together and spend some time alone before and after class. A quiet dinner before or after class will add to the "date."

Adult College Students Ought to Know:

70.   that they should **become involved in campus activities**. Data shows that students who have some degree of involvement in their institutions tend to finish their educational goals. There are campus activities you would enjoy. In addition, you may have experience and expertise, which will be helpful to your classmates.

You may never be in another situation where concerts, ball games, lecture series, and art exhibits will be provided at little or no cost. Take advantage of the things your campus has to offer that extend beyond the classroom.

Adult College Students Ought to Know:

71. that attending college provides you a **great way to meet new friends**. You will have the opportunity to meet other adult students who share your ambitions and dreams. Many people (this author included) found their best friends sitting next to them in a college class. Invite someone to share a cup of coffee or tea at the campus grill. Start a study group. Get a group of fellow adult students and attend campus events together. This is a great time to expand your circle of friends.

Adult College Students Ought to Know:

72. if your institution provides **a lounge for adult students**. Many campuses do. This is a wonderful place to relax, have a cup of coffee, listen to music from your generation, and meet other adult students. In addition, many of these lounges have lockers so that you can store your books. The price you pay to have a locker may be much less than the price you would pay to see someone about the back problems you develop carrying a heavy load of books.

Adult College Students Ought to Know:

73. the importance of **networking with other adult students**. This networking is important for two reasons. One, it will reduce the feeling that you are all alone. Sharing fears and anxieties is valuable. Two, it will give you a source of information about things you don't know. Other students know about child care, financial aid, etc. Learn from them. At many institutions, adult students have formed co-ops so they can share books, rides, skills (such as typing or fixing a car), and child care. Trading child care, cooking, or yard responsibilities with another adult student may be especially helpful during weeks when papers are due or you have lots of exams.

Activity 5
Learning to Juggle Family, Friends, School, and Work

Step One: Using a monthly calendar with blocks large enough to write in, fill in the following:

1. All family activities that are planned for the month. This should include ball games, after-school activities for your children, meetings at school, activities with spouse or significant other, and other predetermined activities.

2. All school assignments for the month. Take each course syllabus and pencil in all due dates for papers, exams, projects, etc.

3.   All work related dates. Do you have major deadlines this month? Are there work projects due?

4.   All activities you have planned with friends.

Note: You may want to use a different color pen or ink for each category.

Step Two: Review the calendar with the following in mind:

1.   Is there a balance in the activities you have planned for family, work, and school?

2.   Is there time for you to relax and rest?

3.   Were there things you wanted to do that can be put off until a later time?

4.   Were some weeks too crowded with deadlines? If so, what can be done ahead of time? What can be rescheduled?

Step Three: Did the time devoted to activities match the priorities in your life? If not, you may need to reconsider how you plan your time and activities.

Adult students often feel pulled between school and family.

Sinking Sounds

A.   ‡I„ll read Psychology right after the end of the Sunday night movie.·

B.   ‡I„m a good typist. I don„t need to learn the computer.·

C.   ‡Let„s sit in the back of the room near the exit so we can leave early and come in late.·

6

Studying Smart

Adult students ought to know that the syllabus is only a guide. Your actual mileage may vary.

Bernis, 56 years old
Computer Science Major

Adult College Students Ought to Know:

74. that the successful students do two things: **go to class and arrive on time**. This advice sounds simple, but college professors will tell you that sometimes the line between failing or passing is whether the student attended class. Those who attend have the chance to ask questions if they don't understand, can impress the professor with their participation, and clarify their notes. Those who arrive on time get seats where they can hear and see. They also impress their professors who will eventually assign their grade.

Helpful Websites:
http://www.academictips.org/acad/sudents-studytips.html
http://www.astrosociety.org/education/resources/success.html
http://www.studynoteshelp.com/

Adult College Students Ought to Know:

75. that they should **designate a place in their homes as their study area**. Choose a quiet, comfortable place to study and do nothing there but study. The benefits of such action should be obvious. Humans are creatures of habit. When we sit at the kitchen table, we immediately think of food. When we lie on our beds, our eyes grow heavy and sleep becomes easier. Therefore, when we choose a place to study and do nothing but study in that area, we will send a message to ourselves and our families that it time for us to study.

Adult College Students Ought to Know:

76. that they must **plan for the unplanned**. Think ahead to the types of emergencies which will cause you difficulties. Now, without the push of a crisis to cloud your thinking, consider the best plan to handle these emergencies. Plan through them and make notes. Then when you receive the call that your child is sick or when the car breaks down, you have an alternate plan already in mind. By having alternative plans with built-in flexibility, you can respond to a stressful situation without compounding it with anxiety over what has to be done.

Adult College Students Ought to Know:

77. that they will receive a **syllabus** from most instructors the first day of class. The syllabus contains the guidelines for the course. It describes the content and goals. It will provide the name of the text to be used. Typically it provides a tentative schedule for the term. Keep your syllabus. Some instructors will not announce test dates if these dates are outlined in the syllabus. By the way, the plural of the word, syllabus, is syllabi.

Helpful Website:
http://homeworktips.about.com/od/preparingforcollege/qt/syllabus.htm

Adult College Students Ought to Know:

78. that they should **keep up with the reading** assigned for each course. Reading before the lectures helps you connect the classroom material to the textbook. If you run out of time, scan. Use post-it notes to mark material in your book that was lectured on by the instructor. You will know that this is information to be given extra attention as you study for a test.

Some students literally color their textbooks by using a variety of highlighters. If all you are doing is turning the white pages of your text from white to blue, yellow, and green, you have accomplished little. The purpose of a highlighter is in its name. It is meant to **highlight** major ideas, key words, etc. If you are highlighting over 20% of the written text, you are not identifying the important ideas.

Adult College Students Ought to Know:

79. the **importance of always practicing good time management**. In fact, effective time management is often the difference between successful students and those who fail. Your time management should focus on three major areas of time – the term, the week, and each day.

Purchase or create a large calendar which will cover the entire school term and put it in a prominent place in your home. Many adult students suggest the refrigerator as the best place to display this calendar. At the beginning of the term, list all family events which will need your attention. Then, using the information found in your syllabi and campus calendar, write in all dates for tests and assignments. Add to the calendar as the term continues. This calendar will give you a quick view of critical periods during the term. If you have two tests and a major paper due one week, you will know to plan family activities for another time. Use different color markers to designate types of activities.

You will also need to keep a daily planner and a daily to-do list. Research has shown that a to-do list is common denominator of all successful people. Find a time each day when you can compose your to-do list. Making the list is not enough. Deciding which of the items should be done first is as important as making the list.

Useful Website:
http://www.academictips.org/acad/timemanagement.html

Adult College Students Ought to Know:

80. the **effective use of transition time**. We all have snatches of time each day when we are waiting for one activity to end or another to begin. This is the time between classes or the time we spend waiting to see our child's doctor. Use this time wisely. Always have material to study with you. The ten minutes you use to scan a chapter or review your notes while waiting in a doctor's office will be ten minutes you have for other activities later. Lunch periods at work are great. An apple and a sandwich can help you get 30-45 minutes of reading or review done. In five days, that adds up.

Adult College Students Ought to Know:

81. the **importance of stopping and asking**, "what is the best use of my time right now?" The answer may be that cuddling your child or snuggling with your spouse is the most important thing you need to do. The answer may be that you need to let the dishes soak or the grass go unmowed while you type a research paper. Ask the question, give an honest answer, and then forget the other things which aren't as important.

Adult College Students Ought to Know:

82. how to **manage big projects**.   A common cause of procrastination is that a task looks so big, we continue to put it off until we have a large block of time. Reality is that you will probably never find that block of time. Therefore, when given a major project, such as a research paper, you should break the task down into smaller pieces. For example, the first step in doing a research paper might be to go to the library to determine what references are available.   Instead of having "work on research paper" on your to-do list, write "check on references in library."   You now have a specific goal and one that can be handled in a limited amount of time.   Once you have your references, you are ready for step two.

Adult College Students Ought to Know:

83. that **libraries have changed**. Arrange for a tour. You will find computer labs for your use. Libraries have become technical centers with access to articles and books online. Many times library resources can be accessed from your home. Because of global connections, students are able to pull data from libraries from all over the world. However, don't forget that librarians want to help you find the materials you need and remain the great resources they have been for decades.

Adult College Students Ought to Know:

84. that **being late to class is unacceptable** except in extreme emergencies. When a student enters late, every eye (all the other students and the instructor) is directed to the person entering. It then takes a few minutes for everyone to get back on track. Repeated patterns of tardiness will create tension between you and the instructor. Plan ahead. Plan to be in class on time.

Adult College Students Ought to Know:

85. that **missing a day of class isn't like missing a day of work**. Many students will go to work when they are sick or when they have something else they would rather do. Yet, too often, these same students will not think twice about missing a class. You should miss class only in an emergency. No one takes notes the way you do. No one hears the instructor the same way you do. A missed class is something that can't be reclaimed.

Know your instructor's attendance policy for each class you are taking. Some instructors count absences against your grade, others do not take attendance but test over their lecture materials. It is important to know your instructor's expectations and what it takes to be successful in each course.

Some institutions require that the grades posted show that failure in a course was a result because of poor attendance. When the reason for failure is because the student failed to come to class, financial support can be eliminated. Understand that not going to class can have repercussions that last a lifetime.

Adult College Students Ought to Know:

86. it is **inappropriate to bring your child to class**. In fact, some institutions have policies that prohibit minors who are not enrolled in the course from attending. If you have an emergency, call your instructor to determine if you have permission to bring your child to class. However, no matter how cute your child might be, your child's presence will not only be a distraction to you, but to other students and to the teacher as well.

Adult College Students Ought to Know:

87. that they should **read their papers aloud** before turning them in to the instructor. If it doesn't make sense to you, it won't make sense to the instructor. Ask a friend or family member to read over papers before giving them to the instructor. Someone more objective will find things you have missed. Always use spell check to check your questions but remember that many common errors will not be found with a spell check program.

Adult College Students Ought to Know:

88. the importance of **sitting in the front of the class**. Sitting in the front of the class sends a message to the instructor that you are interested. Sitting in front of the class eliminates the distractions of less interested students who want to talk and work on other things. Finally, and most importantly, sitting in front of the class puts you in a position where you can see and hear the instructor. This will allow you to not only catch every word but to observe the non-verbal clues the instructor gives about the importance of material.

Adult College Students Ought to Know:

89. that it is **important that the instructor knows who you are**. The instructor should remember who you are because you are always in class, you are always attentive, and you always turn work in on time. Go by the instructor's office if you have a question. Become someone the instructor knows and remembers, not just a name on the roll sheet. Be positively assertive.

Adult College Students Ought to Know:

90. that they should **never be afraid to ask a question**. No question is ever a "dumb" question. If you have a question, other students (especially more traditional age students) will probably have the same question. Therefore, your fellow students will appreciate that you had the courage to ask what they wanted to know. Don't hesitate. Remember, you have paid for the answer.

Adult College Students Ought to Know:

91. your **instructor's names, office hours and location, phone numbers, and e-mail address**. You should also know your instructor's title. Most instructors will tell you how they want to be addressed on the first day of class. Unless told to do so, never address an instructor by his/here first name even if the instructor does remind you of your son, your daughter, or your baby sister. Part-time and adjunct instructors may be difficult to reach so do your best to get phone numbers and e-mail addresses for them. Many academic departments post information about faculty, office hours, etc., on their website.

Adult College Students Ought to Know:

92. that you shouldn't come to class with a **"know it all"** attitude because you feel old enough to be the instructor. The person in charge of the class is the instructor. You will only lose if you try to take over. Don't use the classroom as your personal arena to make pronouncements about the topic being discussed. You are not the authority in the classroom, the instructor is.

Adult students often find it difficult to change roles and become a student once again. Many find it hard to go from being in charge at work or at home to being a student and having someone else tell you what to do. You may feel that you have more practical experience than the instructor. However, you should keep an open mind. There is much to learn in a college classroom. Your instructor and your fellow classmates will all add to your current body of knowledge. Adult students are often surprised at the knowledge brought to the classroom by their more traditional classmates. You are going to school to learn, so enjoy!

Adult College Students Ought to Know:

93.   that they shouldn't take the advice in Item 92 to the extreme. If you have an opinion or experience in a topic, **don't be afraid to share it**. Just be courteous and don't dominate the class. Think, if I were the instructor, what would I want a student to contribute to enhance my lecture?

You also have the right to be respected. If you feel an instructor or a fellow student isn't treating you in a courteous or respectful manner, don't hesitate to say something. Remember to use "I" statements — I think . . . I feel . . . disrespected. This may be unintentional on their part and they often will adjust when you communicate your feeling politely.

Adult College Students Ought to Know:

94. that students will be asked to **demonstrate their knowledge** at a variety of levels. Simply knowing facts, dates, etc., may not assure academic success. You will be asked to comprehend the information. You will be asked to apply the knowledge you have acquired. Be prepared to demonstrate your knowledge at a variety of levels. Therefore, it is important to not just memorize material, but to study so that you will thoroughly understand what is presented in class.

Adult College Students Ought to Know:

95. that they should **study as though they are preparing to take a test**. Since most of what you will be doing on a test is answering questions, you should study by answering the questions you predict will be on the exam. Turn your classroom and text notes into potential test questions and then answer the questions. Buy the study guides which come with your texts and answer the questions provided. Formulate your own questions. You might be surprised how close you come to creating a test which matches that of the instructor.

Adult College Students Ought to Know:

96. that **failure on one test or one assignment does not equate to failure in the course**. Most instructors give several graded assignments. Calmly evaluate why you made a failing grade. Did you study the wrong material? Is there something you didn't understand? Did you make careless mistakes? Did you fail to put your answer in such a way that the instructor understood that you knew the material? If you don't understand why you missed points, go see the instructor. Most importantly, don't give up. Most students find the first test of the term to be the hardest. Remember, more students fail because they simply stop going to class than because they didn't learn the material.

Adult College Students Ought to Know:

97. that sometimes the **best action is to withdraw from a course**. If you discover that you don't have the prerequisites to do well in a course, it may be best to take a step back and get the skills you need. If you have to miss a great deal of classes because of a family emergency, it may be best to withdraw rather than struggle through and fail. Withdrawing doesn't mean you are stopping or that you are a failure. It simply means that for now, being in a particular class is not the wisest action. However, before withdrawing, make sure that doing so does not put your continued enrollment in jeopardy. If you are receiving financial

aid or tuition assistance, check with those offices before withdrawing.

Never assume you will be dropped from a course if you simply stop attending. At most institutions, instructors can't drop students from their rolls. Only the student can initiate the withdrawal process. Therefore, if you don't officially withdraw, the instructor may be forced to give you a failing grade for the term. This may not seem important until you try to re-enroll or transfer to another institution and then discover that your academic record is tarnished by these failing grades.

Adult College Students Ought to Know:

98.   not to be **overzealous about withdrawing from courses**. Some students do it too often. Research your options early by talking with your academic advisor or counselor to determine the appropriate course of action.   Advisors are trained to understand and help with academic problems. Options may be given such as talking with your instructor, seeking tutoring support, or possibly requesting additional time to complete course requirements. Some instructors will issue an "incomplete" grade while you finish course requirements.   Other terminology or options may be used at your institution but what's important is trained advisors are available to help. Use them.

Adult College Students Ought to Know:

99. your **attitude is the key barometer of your success**. You start like gang busters, highly motivated and focused. Then, you encounter course work that takes time away from things you've always enjoyed doing, or your family and friends put undue expectations on you. It is easy to get discouraged. The key point is PERSIST. Those who persist in spite of obstacles will graduate. Those who don't persist, return to their former lives and never move forward to meeting their needs.

Always remember that you are an intelligent, industrious, motivated, and energetic person who wants to make your life better for yourself and those around you. You can DO it!

Activity 6
Making Molehills Out of Mountains

Select a task that seems very large and still is not due for a few more weeks. Take that task and break it down into its component parts.

Example: Term paper for English 101

1.   Select a topic
2.   Research the topic
3.   Make outline from notes
4.   Make a rough draft
5.   Write paper
6.   Proof by self and someone else
7.   Re-write final draft

Once you've broken the task down into smaller components, decide a deadline for each component. Don't think of the entire task, just concentrate on accomplishing the task by the deadline you've established. Soon you will be at the top of the mountain with a completed project in hand.

Project Title _____   Completion Date _____

Step 1.   _____   _____

Step 2.   _____   _____

Step 3.   _____   _____

Step 4.   _____   _____

Step 5.   _____   _____

Step 6.   _____   _____

Step 7.   _____   _____

Long term goals can become a reality that everyone will enjoy forever.

Using Technology to Your Advantage

E-mail and the World Wide Web are not from a Star Wars movie. They'll connect you to the world and to campus services

George, 40 years old
History Major

Adult College Students Ought to Know:

100.   that it will be impossible to be successful in higher education without a basic **knowledge of technology**. Even if you aren't enrolled in online courses, your professors will often enhance the class through online assignments, discussion boards, and resources. Faculty and administrators will communicate with you through e-mail and online announcements. You will register for courses via the Internet. Therefore, you will find it impossible to function in the higher education environment without basic computer knowledge.

Adult College Students Ought to Know:

101.   that it is critical that you have a **basic knowledge of computers and word processing**. If you don't feel comfortable with creating documents on the computer or using the computer to communicate, it would be best to take a class to learn some basic computer skills before enrolling in college level courses. Check with a local university to see if a continuing education course is available at minimum cost. You will find this small investment will be pay large dividends as you earn your degree.

Adult College Students Ought to Know:

102.   that **much of the information you will need to manage your degree can be found online**. Review the website for the university, college, and department in which you will enroll. Typically you will find information concerning your degree, admission requirements, important deadlines, registration, and how to order a transcript. Checking the website often will reduce a great deal of frustration.

Adult College Students Ought to Know:

103.   that you may need to **purchase computer equipment or upgrade your computer equipment** before taking classes. Before buying a computer or upgrading your current computer, talk to your advisor to determine what he/she would recommend. Most online courses require a specific hardware configuration to function in the course. Some majors (like education or art) require a particular operating system in order to run the software you will need for courses. If you are purchasing a computer, consider a laptop so that you can take it to class. The good news is that some institutions provide laptops to their students. Before purchasing a computer or upgrading your current computer, find out if you will be provided a computer by the institution.

Adult College Students Ought to Know:

104.   that **courtesy** is needed as you use computer equipment. If you take your computer to class, remember the computer is there to allow you to take notes or to access resources from your instructor. It is not there to allow you to check and answer e-mails, play games, or work on other assignments. Your professor will not be pleased to hear, "You have mail," during the lecture.

This advice also applies to your cell phone. Phones should be on vibrate during class and you should only leave to take a message if there is an emergency. Texting during class is never appropriate. Texting is becoming the number one frustrations for faculty. Don't be the student that contributes to this frustration.

Adult College Students Ought to Know:

105.   that the faculty, staff, and administration of your institution **will communicate with you through e-mail**. You will either be expected to provide an e-mail address to the institution or you will be provided an e-mail by the institution. Check this e-mail often. Yes, you will receive lots of junk mail but you also will receive important notices concerning advisement and pre-registration opportunities, graduation information, and class notices from faculty. Some institutions are now providing campus e-mail addresses that continue after you graduate. Therefore, you can continue to receive alumni information and announcements about what is happening at the institution.

Adult College Students Ought to Know:

106.   that **caution is needed when you communicate** with faculty and fellow students through online chats, discussion boards, or e-mail. Be sure you have carefully read what you wrote before hitting the "send" button. A wrong word or missing word can change the meaning of your message. It is wise to check your spelling and grammar before sending the message.

When e-mailing, don't reply to "all" unless you want everyone listed to get the message. Remember that e-mails can be reviewed and shared by those you had not intended. Before sending an e-mail that might have a negative impact on you academically, have someone else read the content.

Helpful Websites:
http://www.emailreplies.com/
http://owl.english.purdue.edu/owl/resource/636/01/

Adult College Students Ought to Know:

107.   that **plagiarizing and cheating** may be easier via the computer. However, the same sources that you can easily find and paste into your work can be found by your professors. Just as you would not copy written material without giving the proper reference, do not cut and paste from internet resources unless you appropriately reference the material.

Helpful Website:
http://www.library.cornell.edu/olinuris/ref/research/webcrit.html

Adult College Students Ought to Know:

108.   that **not all websites are equal in their accuracy** or are appropriate as a resource for college level work. Only use websites from reputable organizations. If anyone can post to the site, it may mean that no one is checking the information for accuracy. Your professors may not accept some websites as valid resources for your assignments. Have this conversation with your professors.

Adult College Students Ought to Know:

109.   that while **online classes** are a valuable resource for adult students, they require a basic level of computer knowledge and for you to be motivated to complete the work. Before enrolling in an online course, talk to others who have taken online classes about the advantages and disadvantages. Find out how assignments are submitted and the amount of time expected for completing the work. Contrary to popular myths, valid online courses take the same or more time commitment than face-to-face classes. Online courses typically require 9 to 12 hours per week for a three-hour course but can require an even greater commitment of time.

Adult College Students Ought to Know:

110.   that there is a difference between **online courses and computer-enhanced courses**. When taking an online course, all work and interactions occur via the Internet. Typically, the student will not come to campus nor will the student meet the teacher. Often, students and teachers work and live in different parts of the country or world.

Computer-enhanced classes still meet in a classroom. The instructor and students work together. The instructor may post information on a website or course portal to enhance the lectures. The syllabus might be posted online. In some cases, students take their exams online.

Adult College Students Ought to Know:

111.   that you should use caution as you use **social networks** such as Facebook or My Space. Faculty can access these sites and can see remarks you make about them or their courses. Future employers can access the information you put online and this can be helpful or harmful as you look for a job. Remember that the worldwide web is called that because you will be sharing information worldwide. Unless you are willing to share information about yourself with the world, don't put it online.

Helpful Websites:

http://webtrends.about.com/od/socialnetworking/a/socialnetwork_b.htm

http://www.pbs.org/mediashift/2007/08/your-guide-to-social-networking-online241.html

Adult College Students Ought to Know:

112. that technology has advanced beyond word processing and e-mail. Today students are asked to produce PowerPoint presentations, create websites, run software, and create blogs. Many professors provide lectures via **podcasting** and require students to produce their own podcasting. Podcasting is a convenient way to access materials and lectures.

Using new technologies can be stressful but the stress produced by learning new skills is worth the effort. The technology skills you learn will serve you well in your personal life and in your career

Helpful Website:
http://www.educause.edu/GuideToPodcasting

Activity 7
Computer Skills Self Assessment

Word Processing	Very Skilled	Some Knowledge	No Knowledge
1. I can efficiently type on a a computer keyboard.	_____	_____	_____
2. I can create and save a document.	_____	_____	_____
3. I can cut, copy, and paste text in a document.	_____	_____	_____
4. I can create folders on my computer with which to organize my work.	_____	_____	_____

Word Processing	Very Skilled	Some Knowledge	No Knowledge
5. I can use spell-check, the thesaurus, and page formatting.	_____	_____	_____
6. I can print a document.	_____	_____	_____
7. I can create a bulleted or numbered list.	_____	_____	_____
8. I can insert a picture or object into my document.	_____	_____	_____
9. I can change the font type and size.	_____	_____	_____

The Internet	Very Skilled	Some Knowledge	No Knowledge
1. I can search for material using search engines such as Google or Bing.	_____	_____	_____
2. I can disable pop-up blockers.	_____	_____	_____
3. I can copy material to use in material.	_____	_____	_____
4. I know how to properly reference material found on the Web.	_____	_____	_____
5. I can bookmark a Website.	_____	_____	_____
6. I can download files from the Internet.	_____	_____	_____

E-mail	**Very Skilled**	**Some Knowledge**	**No Knowledge**
1. I can create an e-mail message.	_____	_____	_____
2. I can attach pictures or other files to my e-mail messages.	_____	_____	_____
3. I can send an e-mail message to multiple recipients	_____	_____	_____
4. I can reply to or forward messages.	_____	_____	_____
5. I can open and save e-mail attachments.	_____	_____	_____

Operation Systems	Very Skilled	Some Knowledge	No Knowledge
1. I can open multiple files.	_____	_____	_____
2. I can insert and remove a flash drive, and open and save files to it.	_____	_____	_____
3. I can use a mouse to navigate information on the computer.	_____	_____	_____
4. I know how to use the space bar, return key, enter key, delete key, and backspace key.	_____	_____	_____
5. I can download and install appropriate programs and plug-ins to my computer.	_____	_____	_____

It you marked the majority of the items as "Very Skilled," you should be able to manage the requirements for most college level courses that use the computer for all or part of the course.

If you marked the majority of the items as "Some Knowledge," you should talk to your advisor or the instructor of the course before enrolling in a course to determine of your skills are sufficient for the course.

If you marked the majority of the items as "No Knowledge," you should investigate non-college level courses (such as continuing education) to learn the computer skills you will need to be successful.

Conclusion

Ultimately, *you* are in charge of your own education. College officials aren't mind readers; they need you to tell them what you need. Each year colleges and universities spend more and more money trying to fine-tune their services for adult learners but the task is overwhelming. Why? It is because adult learners are more diverse and complex when compared to traditional age students. Therefore, it is important that you tell college and university administrators what you and other adult students need to adjust, persist, and graduate from college. By verbalizing your needs, you will enhance your own educational experience and the experiences of those that follow you.

Now that you've read this book, the real work starts. It is time to effectively manage your dream of earning a degree. Sure it will be tough and there will be days you will want to give up. There will be times when it will require adjustments by you and those that love you. Your advantage is your adjustment skills may be more advanced and mature than traditional age students. Conversely, you have more responsibility that needs to be carried along with you during this adjustment. You will struggle daily to balance your goals and these responsibilities. Such struggles define you as a dependable adult and give you the strength to carry through with your goals.

I wish you success in your journey as many wished me success in mine, and I hope you will use the ideas in this book to promote your success. Use it as a constant reference and keep it with you in your journey through this adjustment in your life. Use the Glossary of College Terms to learn the lingo of college. You may find additional ideas in the first book in this series, *100 Things Every College Freshman Ought to Know*.

While this book is written with a more traditional student frame of reference, it contains valuable advice for all students, including adult learners.

In my career as a college professor and administrator, I have had the opportunity to work with thousands of adult students. I have shared the sadness of students who had to delay their academic goals to deal with family and/or work responsibilities, and have rejoiced when they returned to complete their degrees. I have watched students struggle academically as they began their course work and joined in the celebration when they graduated with honors. I have gained strength and courage from their persistence. And because of these students, I know that long term goals can become reality when students have a vision of what they want from life. Good luck in making your dreams come true.

One last thought:

Participate in your graduation.   You have earned the right to walk proudly across the stage and receive your degree.   Family and friends who have suported you have the right to celebrate your success with you. You have made it, so celebrate.   And start thinking about the next degree!!!

Dr. Carlette Hardin

P.S. My goal is to help make the college transition process easier for you and others. If you discover "things" that you think would help future students, would you let me know? An Editorial Contributions card is at the end or, as you perfect your e-mail skills, forward to Cambridges@aol.com. THANKS.

Glossary of College Terms

Academic year. The period of time from the beginning of class in the fall and the date of graduation in the spring.

Accreditation. Recognition by an accrediting organization of a college, university, or a study program, for meeting specified minimum standards of quality in its instruction, staffing, facilities, financial stability, and policies.

Achievement or Assessment Tests. Tests in specific college preparatory subjects. Required by some colleges for admission and used also in course placement.

Adjunct Faculty. Visiting or part-time instructors.

Admission. Acceptance of a student for enrollment to a college or a specific degree program.

Advising. The offering of advice, opinion, or instruction given to students, usually by an assigned advisor. Career, academic, financial aid are the most common types involving adult students.

Alumnus and (Alumni, pl.). A graduate from a school or college.

Articulation Agreement. An agreement between two institutions of higher education which outlines what course work will transfer between the institutions. Typically these are agreements between community colleges and four-year institutions to ease the transfer of students from the two-year institution to the four-year institution.

Associate degree. The degree granted by a college or for completion of a study program normally taking two years of full-time study (or longer, in part-time study).

Audit. To take a course without credit. Student is not required to take an exam nor submit work for review.

Baccalaureate or Bachelor's degree. A degree granted for completing a course of study usually requiring 120-128 semester credits, (often called a 4-year degree program).

Bursar. The administrator responsible for billings and collections of tuition and fees.

Career services office or center. A college office or department providing services to assist students in choosing careers, in developing skills in searching and qualifying for jobs, and in actually finding and obtaining jobs. The office provides listings of job openings and interviews with corporate and government recruiters visiting the campus. Such an office might also be identified as a placement bureau, student placement office, or career resources center.

Catalog. A document outlining the academic programs, policies, procedures, and course descriptions of an institution. Typically, catalogs cover the policies for a particular year. Catalogs may be published in book form or be an electronic document. This document is sometimes called the university bulletin.

Certificate. A credential issued by the college or university in recognition of completion of curriculum other than one leading to a degree or diploma.

Challenge examinations. Examinations offered by a college that are prepared in specific subjects by its own faculty members and that enable students to earn credits by passing the examinations instead of attending class sessions.

CLEP (College-Level Examination Program). CLEP consists of a series of examinations in 33 areas that test an individual's college-level knowledge gained through life experiences. Many colleges grant credit to students who meet a score identified by the institution.

Closed sections. A section or course that has been filled to capacity; no further registrations will be accepted without signed permission by the instructor.

Commencement. The graduation ceremonies held at the end of the term at which time associate and bachelor degrees are awarded by the university.

Computer-enhanced courses. Courses that meet in a traditional format but which have much of the course content provided through the Internet.

Concentration. A particular emphasis within a major area.

Corequisites.   A course that must be or can be taken concurrently with a given course.

Correspondence study course. A course for which the student registers and receives and sends course materials by mail, and in which the student learns independently without class attendance. Before enrolling in such courses, students should check to make sure the credits will be accepted by their institutions.

Course. A specific subject of study.

Curriculum. The formal education requirements necessary to qualify for a degree, diploma, or certificate.

Dean's List. The published list of undergraduate students who have achieved an honors grade average (3.5 or higher) for the semester.

Department. A unit of the school's faculty organized to provide courses of study in a specific discipline such as English, Biology or Computer Science.

Developmental Courses. Developmental skills courses are designed for students who need additional basic skills training or academic preparation to enable them to succeed in regular college-level courses or programs.

Discipline. An area of study representing a branch of knowledge, such as mathematics.

Distance Education. Learners in remote locations meet at a site that has cable or satellite receivers, phone lines, and video cameras so that one or two-way video contact is provided with an instructor.

Division. A group of related academic disciplines, such as the social sciences; the arts and the humanities; and the biological and physical science.

Drop. To cancel one's registration for a particular course. An option available only during a specific time frame after the semester begins.

Elective course. A course that a student takes by choice as distinguished from a course specifically required for a degree.

Electronic registration. Course registration via the computer or telephone.

Federal Direct Subsidized and Unsubsidized Consolidation Loans. A federally sponsored program of financial aid in which students may take out loans for college costs at subsidized interest rates, and for which financial need is an eligibility requirement.

Federal Pell Grant. Pell Grants are awarded only to undergraduate students who have not earned a bachelor's or professional degree. Unlike a loan, a Pell Grant doesn't have to be repaid.

Federal Perkins Loans. A low-interest loan for both undergraduate and graduate students with exceptional financial need. The loan is made with government funds with a share contributed by the school. This loan must be repaid.

Federal Supplemental Educational Opportunity Grants. A Federal Supplemental Educational Opportunity Grant is for undergraduates with exceptional financial need. An FSEOG doesn't have to be paid back.

Federal Work-Study (FWS). A federally sponsored financial aid program that provides jobs for students with demonstrated financial need.

Financial need. The difference between what the student and her/his spouse (or parents) can afford to spend toward the student's college costs and the total of those costs, as computed in the need analysis systems used by colleges and other aid sponsors. In those systems, colleges and other sponsors require aid applicants to complete family financial information collection forms to provide basic data for the computations.

Free Application for Federal Student Aid (FAFSA). A form that may be used by students applying for federally sponsored financial aid for college students, chiefly Pell Grants and Guaranteed Student Loans.

General Education Courses. Courses designed to help students discover the relatedness of knowledge and acquire a core of information, attitudes and capabilities basic to their formal college education and their continuing education throughout life.

Graduate Student. A student who has received a bachelor's degree and has met all criteria for admission into the Graduate School.

Graduate study program, graduate degree. A study program for which a bachelor's degree or the equivalent is usually required for admission; a degree earned through a graduate study program.

Incomplete. A grade given by the instructors to indicate a student is in good standing but could not finish the class because of circumstances beyond his/her control. A grade of incomplete is only an option if the instructor agrees to assign it and must be removed within a period of time established by the institution.

Independent Study. A program that does not require class attendance for degree credit. The student learns independently under the supervision of a faculty member.

Interdisciplinary Courses. Those which deal with two or more academic subjects/disciplines (i.e., psychology and education).

Liberal Arts. The broad scope of academic disciplines consisting of the humanities, the social sciences, and the natural sciences.

Lower-Division Courses. Introductory courses usually taken during the first two years of college study.

Major. The subject or career field that serves as the area of concentration in the student's study program for a degree. For a bachelor's degree, students must commonly earn about one-fourth of their credits in the major.

Matriculated Student. An enrolled student who has been accepted through the Admissions Office as a degree candidate.

Mid-Term. The halfway point of a semester.

Minor. A secondary concentration in a specific discipline or field of study, usually requiring about half the number of credits required for a major.

Non-Degree Seeking Student. A non-degree student taking one or more credit courses for personal or professional development. These courses do not count toward a degree. Non-degree seeking students are not eligible for financial aid.

Ombudsperson. The administrative officer at some colleges whose major duties are to receive and rectify grievances reported by students.

Online Courses. Course material that is delivered through the Internet.

Orientation. Activities and programs designed to help the new student become acquainted with the university.

Pass-Fail Option. A provision allowing students to take a course on a pass or fail basis, rather than receiving a letter grade. PASS-FAIL is then excluded in computing a student's grade-point average (GPA). Students should always check with their advisor when considering the P/F option.

Permanent Record. The card on which the Registrar lists all of a student's courses, semester hours credited, grades, status, and certain personal information.

Placement Tests. Tests given by College departments which determine a student's level of proficiency in a particular subject area. These tests are used to place students in classes at the appropriate level for their abilities.

Podcasting. The recording of internet radio or similar internet audio program which are then downloaded to an iPod or other portable digital audio device for review at a later time.

Probation (Academic). When a student's GPA falls below 2.0 for a given semester or his/her cumulative GPA is below 2.0, a conditional status will be given to the student; academic probation should be considered a warning as well as an opportunity to improve.

Prerequisite. Knowledge, skills, or coursework that must be completed before enrolling in a particular course.

Proficiency Examination Program (PEP). A program of examinations in undergraduate college subjects widely used by colleges to award degree credit to students by examination, and offered by the American College Testing Program.

Quarter Hours. The unit of credit used by schools on quarter term plans.

Registrar. The college administrator responsible for supervising course enrollment, academic recording, and certification.

Registration. The process by which the student chooses, enrolls in, and pays for course sessions for the term: also, the period of several days before the term opening designated by the college for carrying out that process.

Requirements. (1) For a college degree, the amounts and kinds of study stipulated by the college as necessary in order to qualify for that degree. (2) For college admission, the documents, test results, and possibly minimum qualifications and interview, stipulated by the college as necessary in order to qualify for admission.

Schedule. The courses for which a student is enrolled during a semester or summer term.

Semester. Half an academic year: 15-16 weeks.

Semester Hours. The unit of credit used by schools on semester plans.

Student Identification Number. An identification number developed for each student by the institution. This number is used on all institutional records.

Survey Course. A course designed to provide a general overview of an area of study.

Syllabus. An outline of topics to be covered by the instructor including assignments to be completed by students during a course.

Terminal study program. A study program usually offered by a two-year community college that is designed to qualify students for immediate employment upon completing the program rather than for transfer to a bachelor's degree program; many terminal programs lead to an associate degree.

Transcript. An official record of the courses taken and grades earned by a student throughout high school or in one or more colleges.

Transfer. Admission to a new school with acceptance of previously earned credits toward the degree, diploma, certificate, or program requirements of the new school.

Transfer Credit. Credit accepted by a college toward a degree on the basis of prior study by the student at another college.

Transfer Program. A study program usually offered by a two-year community college that is designed to qualify students completing the program for transfer to a bachelor's degree program with little or no loss of credit; most transfer programs lead to an associate degree.

Trimester. An alternate name for semester employed by colleges that offer year-round study. Three trimesters make up one year (with the third trimester representing their summer sessions).

Tuition. The amount of money charged to students for instructional services (course fees).

Undergraduate. Pertaining to studies for associate or bachelor's degrees.

Upper Division. Courses at the level of the junior and senior years of study for a bachelor's degree.

Web-based Courses. Courses offered via the Internet.

Weekend College Study Program. A study program designed especially for working adults in which students attend course sessions primarily or entirely during weekends.

Withdrawal. A release from enrollment. A student may usually withdraw from a course officially within a specified period without being graded. Withdrawal without permission may result in a failing grade.

Sources:
Financial Aid Glossary
http://colleges.collegetoolkit.com/guides/financial-aid/reglossary.aspx
Various university catalogs and bulletins

Nurse's aide, Cindy: "Is college tough?"

Nurse's aide, Sandra: "Not really! What's tough is saying 'No' to the kids, my husband, my supervisor, and telling my family I won't have Thanksgiving dinner!"

Editorial Comments and Contribution Pages

Dear Reader,

Your comments can help other adult college students make a smoother transition to college. Please share your thoughts, ideas, and suggestions on the following pages or on a separate sheet of paper. Also, fill in the biographical information below. I'll include a special reference by-line in my next edition to acknowledge all contributors. Thank you!

Name _____

Institution _____

City _____ State _____ Zip _____

☐ *Student*
☐ *Faculty*
☐ *Administrator*
☐ *Family/Friend*
☐ _____

(Cut or tear out form or e-mail to Cambridges@aol.com)

My thoughts, ideas, and suggestions are

_____

_____

_____

_____

_____

_____

_____

_____

_____

_____

_____

(Cut or tear out form or e-mail to Cambridges@aol.com)

_____

_____

_____

_____

_____

_____

_____

_____

Mail To: Dr. Carlette Jackson Hardin
             c/o The Cambridge Stratford Study Skills Institute
             8560 Main Street
             Williamsville, NY 14221

(Cut or tear out form or e-mail to Cambridges@aol.com)

Phone Chat

How's college going?

Oh, it's great. I'm getting very time oriented.
fi I walk the dog with my head phones on playing
*   Psychology 101,*
fi the kids and I go to the library together,
fi and when Herb complains of road rage, I simply
*   say, 'How does that make you feel?'*

Works Consulted

Christ, F. L., & Ganey, L. (2007). *100 things every online student ought to know* (2nd ed). Williamsville, NY: Cambridge Stratford Study Skills Institute.

Hardin, C. (2008). Adult students in higher education: A portrait of transitions. In B. Barefoot (Ed.). *The first year and beyond: Rethinking the challenge of collegiate transition*. San Francisco: Jossey Bass.

Knowles, M. S. (1980). *The modern practice of adult education: From pedagogy to andragogy*. Englewood Cliffs: Prentice Hall/Cambridge.

Knowles, M. S., et al. (1984). *Andragogy in action: Applying modern principles of adult education*. San Francisco: Jossey-Bass.

Schmidt, G. (2008). *The busy adult's guide to making college happen*. Chappaqua, NY: Break Free Publishing.

Siebert, A., & Darr, M. (2008). *The adult student's guide to survival and success* (6th ed). Portland: Practical Psychology Press, Inc.

Upcraft, M.L., & Gardner, J.N. (1989). *The freshman year experience*. San Francisco: Jossey-Bass.

Webliography
A list of web sites referenced in each chapter.

Chapter 1 Getting Started

http://nces.ed.gov/programs/digest/d09/tables/dt09_191.asp
National Center for Education Statistics

http://www.ecampustours.com/forparents/collegeplanning/
adviceforadultstudents.htm
e-campus tours

http://www.ehow.com/how_2081881_audit-class.html
How to Audit a Class

http://www.collegeview.com/articles/CV/application/two-vs-four-years.html
College View

http://www.collegeconfidential.com/dean/archives/000294.htm
College Dean Ò Ask for Advice

http://collegesearch.collegeboard.com/search/adv_typeofschool.jsp
College Board

http://www.accreditedonlinecolleges.com/
Accredited Online Degree

http://ope.ed.gov/accreditation/
The Database of Accredited Postsecondary Institutions and Programs

http://www.back2college.com/library/test.htm
Back to College

http://www.collegescholarships.org/blog/2009/04/29/getting-college-credit-for-life-experience-it-can-be-done/
College Scholarships

http://professionals.collegeboard.com/higher-ed/placement/clep/advise/adult-students
Advising Adult Students

http://www.nontradstudents.com/
The Non-Traditional Student

http://adulted.about.com/od/intro/u/Nontradstudentpath.htm
About.com

http://www.adultstudentcenter.com/
Adult Student Center
http://www.collegeforadults.org/
College for Adults

Chapter 2 Understanding the Definitions and Customs

http://www.collegeview.com/articles/CV/campuslife/
academic_advisor.html
Your Academic Advisor

http://www.completecollegeplanning.net/what-to-ask-your-academic-
adviser.php
College Planning

http://www.back2college.com/gpa.htm
Calculate Your GPA

http://www.youtube.com/watch?v=VhLMTaExzOs
How to Calculate GPA

http://www.smartaboutcollege.org/get-to-college/college-degree-types.jsp
Smart about College

http://www.online-degrees-today.com/content/types-of-college-degrees-online.shtml
Types of College Degrees

http://www.bachelordegrees.net/bachelor/types-of-degrees.asp
Types of Bachelor's Degrees

Chapter 4 Reaching Out

http://www.back2college.com/library/finad.htm
Back to College: Financial Aid

http://www.braintrack.com/financial-aid-articles/articles/non-traditional-students
Financial Aid for Non-Traditional Students

http://www.gibill.va.gov/
Department of Veterans Affairs

http://www.collegescholarships.org/scholarships/veterans.htm
College Scholarships for Veterans

http://www2.ed.gov/programs/triovub/index.html
Veterans Upward Bound Program

http://www2.ed.gov/about/offices/list/ocr/transition.html
Students with Disabilities Preparing for Postsecondary Education

http://www.educationquest.org/swd.asp
College Planning for Students with Disabilitie

Chapter 6 Studying Smart

http://www.academictips.org/acad/sudents-studytips.html
Student to Student Study Tips

http://www.astrosociety.org/education/resources/success.html
Hints on How to Succeed in College Classes

http://www.studynoteshelp.com/
Study Tips for Students

http://homeworktips.about.com/od/preparingforcollege/qt/syllabus.htm
What is a Syllabus?

http://www.academictips.org/acad/timemanagement.html
Time Management Tips

Chapter 7 Using Technology to Your Advantage

http://www.emailreplies.com/
Email Etiquette

http://owl.english.purdue.edu/owl/resource/636/01/
Email Etiquette

http://www.library.cornell.edu/olinuris/ref/research/webcrit.html
Five Criteria for Evaluating Web Pages

http://webtrends.about.com/od/socialnetworking/a/socialnetwork_b.htm
Social Networking Guide for Beginners

http://www.pbs.org/mediashift/2007/08/your-guide-to-social-networking-online241.html
Your Guide to Social Networking

http://www.educause.edu/GuideToPodcasting
Guide to Podcasting

Index by Item Number

About the Publisher
The Cambridge Stratford Study Skills Institute

Cambridge Stratford, Ltd. formed The Cambridge Stratford Study Skills Institute in 1985 with the help of its current president, Peter W. Stevens, a former vice president from a private college in New York. It is an international organization of learning and study skills specialists and tutor training professionals dedicated to helping students of all ages to STUDY SMARTER, READ FASTER and SCORE HIGHER ON TESTS, key ingredients for success in school as well as in life.

Cambridge Stratford Study Skills Course System

The CSSS INSTITUTE provides teacher and tutor training services, private courses for students in summer and after school programs nationally, and publishes the internationally renowned study skills curriculum entitled **The Cambridge Stratford Study Skills Course**. It is taught publicly by schools, colleges, federal and state grant programs at 3 levels (6–8th: 20 hour edition, 9–11th: 30 hour edition, and 12–15th: 10 hour edition, entitled *Ten Tips for Academic Success*, available in English and Spanish). These editions include 4 components; Student Workbook, Teacher Manual, Transparency/CD Set and Listening Tape Set.

Tutor Training Research Study

In 1994, The INSTITUTE introduced a research-based tutor training curriculum nationally under the direction of Dr. Ross MacDonald entitled *The Master Tutor: A Guidebook for More Effective Tutoring*. It includes the state-of-the-art methods tutors can use to improve the effectiveness of one-on-one tutoring sessions and consists of a self-instructional Guidebook for tutors, a Tutor

Trainer's Manual, and Transparency/CD Set. A pre- and post-assessment, **The TESAT** (Tutor Evaluation and Self-Assessment Tool) is available for validating improved tutoring skills.

Starting 2002-2003, the *Online eMaster Tutor Training Course* was introduced to assist tutor trainers in training peer and staff tutors online. A train-the-trainer course, the *Online eMaster Tutor Trainer's Course*, was also made available to train online instructors in effectively teaching tutors using a hybrid of face-to-face and online instructional components.

Improving the Retention of College Students

The CSSS INSTITUTE's mission is to help students prepare for and succeed in college. This second edition of *100 Things Every Adult College Student Ought to Know* represents its further effort to help adult college-bound students adjust to the difficult transition required in becoming a successful college student. It is a suggested reading for every adult planning to start college for the first time, as well as those who may be returning to college after a lapse in time. Colleges may find it helpful in their retention-management efforts since it helps adult students understand college customs, practices, vocabulary, and procedures, plus includes important tips for balancing responsibilities in college, family, and work environments.. In addition to this new edition for adult college students, four other self-orientation to college books have been published to help traditional, online learners, international students, and students with a disability adjust to the difficult transitions required in becoming a successful college student. These navigation-to-college guidebooks, ***100 Things Every Freshman Ought to Know, 100 Things Every Online Student Ought to Know, 100 Things Every International Student Ought to Know*** and ***100 Things Every College Student With a Disability Ought to Know*** are suggested reading for all those starting college for the first time as well as those who may be returning to college after a lapse in time. Pre college and college preparation programs may find them helpful in building college persistence and retention among their students since each assists students in understanding college customs, practices, vocabulary, and procedures, plus each includes important tips for balancing responsibilities in college, family, and work environments.

NOTE: Prospective Authors — The *100 Things* series can be expanded to help others. If you have an idea, book, or concept that might help students succeed in school or college, please contact us at the address on the next page or via e-mail. We're interested!

If you need information about any of the products or services offered or would like a sample lesson (PREVIEW MANUAL) forwarded for your review, write or call today.

The Cambridge Stratford Study Skills Institute
8560 Main Street
Williamsville, New York 14221
(716) 626-9044 or FAX (716) 626-9076
Cambridges@aol.com
http://www.cambridgestratford.com

*"Experienced travelers know that in order to get the most out of a journey, it's a good idea to consult a travel guide for information about the customs, language, and resources needed to make the most of their time and money. Dr. Hardin's **100 Things Every Adult College Student Ought to Know** provides adult students with the travel savvy necessary to make their college educational journey less rocky."*

Dr. Carolyn Hopper
Study Skills Coordinator
Middle Tennessee State University

*"**100 Things Every Adult College Student Ought to Know** provides potential and current students a useful guide as they embark upon thier path to lifelong learning. By utilizing practical information and exercises, Dr. Hardin helps to eliminate the fears and apprehensions of the adult student. The diversity of information is applicable for all levels and types of education and training programs. This book is a 'must' for all adult learner programs."*

Marius "Gabe" DeGabriele
Executive Director, Association for
Non-Traditional Students in
Higher Education (ANTSHE)

__100 Things Every Adult College Student Ought to Know__ offers adult students a compass and a navigation map for the murky waters of a college campus. It provides the vocabulary, the questions to ask, decision making assistance, and tips to enable adult students to be relieved of the fears associated with setting foot on campus.

Having worked with adult students for a number of years as the coordinator of an adult high school, my colleagues and I often talked of how to support mature students attending school. This book is exactly what we had in mind."

Susan Simms, Ed. D.
Former Coordinator – Cohn Adult High School
Nashville, TN

*The new second edition of **100 Things Every Adult College Student Ought to Know** has been delicately updated and revised by Dr. Hardin that proves more meaningful and helpful to adults. For example, by adding a new Chapter on using technology she brings adults further ahead in adjusting to current college learning and the expectations of professors. Helpful web sites tied tocertain items also expand assistance. Plus, more emphasis on Financial Aid and the importance of involving family and friends in your choice for college is readily apparent. Three cheers for making this "must read book" for adult learner programs a greater "must."*

Tom Rowland
Project Director, Commonwealth Educational
Opportunity Center
NEOCA President